EXPLORING MINERALS

MINERALOGISTS AT WORK!

ELSIE OLSON

Consulting Editor, Diane Craig, M.A./Reading Specialist

Super Sandcastle

An Imprint of Abdo Publishing
abdopublishing.com

abdopublishing.com

Published by Abdo Publishing, a division of ABDO, PO Box 398166, Minneapolis, Minnesota 55439. Copyright © 2018 by Abdo Consulting Group, Inc. International copyrights reserved in all countries. No part of this book may be reproduced in any form without written permission from the publisher. Super SandCastle™ is a trademark and logo of Abdo Publishing.

Printed in the United States of America, North Mankato, Minnesota

102017
012018

THIS BOOK CONTAINS RECYCLED MATERIALS

Design: Kelly Doudna, Mighty Media, Inc.
Production: Mighty Media, Inc.
Editor: Jessie Alkire
Cover Photographs: iStockphoto; NASA; Wikimedia Commons
Interior Photographs: iStockphoto; NASA; Science Source; Shutterstock; Wikimedia Commons

Publisher's Cataloging-in-Publication Data

Names: Olson, Elsie, author.
Title: Exploring minerals: mineralogists at work! / by Elsie Olson.
Other titles: Mineralogists at work!
Description: Minneapolis, Minnesota : Abdo Publishing, 2018. | Series: Earth detectives |
Identifiers: LCCN 2017946513 | ISBN 9781532112317 (lib.bdg.) | ISBN 9781614799733 (ebook)
Subjects: LCSH: Mineralogy--Juvenile literature. | Minerals--Juvenile literature. |
    Occupations--Juvenile literature. | Earth sciences--Juvenile literature.
Classification: DDC 549--dc23
LC record available at https://lccn.loc.gov/2017946513

Super SandCastle™ books are created by a team of professional educators, reading specialists, and content developers around five essential components—phonemic awareness, phonics, vocabulary, text comprehension, and fluency—to assist young readers as they develop reading skills and strategies and increase their general knowledge. All books are written, reviewed, and leveled for guided reading, early reading intervention, and Accelerated Reader™ programs for use in shared, guided, and independent reading and writing activities to support a balanced approach to literacy instruction.

CONTENTS

WHAT IS A MINERAL?

A mineral is a natural **substance**. It is nonliving. Minerals are solids. Minerals are made of one or more elements. Earth has more than 4,000 types of minerals!

Minerals form rocks. Some rocks have many minerals. Others are just one mineral. Minerals have a crystal structure. This is the way a mineral's elements are arranged. Each mineral has a **unique** structure.

WHO STUDIES MINERALS?

Some scientists study minerals. These scientists are mineralogists. They perform tests. These tests help identify minerals.

This work is important. Minerals have many purposes. You use minerals every day! Salt is a mineral. So is fluorite. This is in toothpaste!

Fluorite

Most mineralogists work for universities. Others work for governments, mining companies, or museums.

FRIEDRICH MOHS

Friedrich Mohs was a mineralogist. He was born in Germany in the 1700s. Mohs studied many science topics in college. He also began studying minerals.

Mohs moved to Austria in 1802. He worked for a mineral collector. Mohs identified minerals. He organized them too. Scientists did not yet have a system to organize minerals. So, Mohs made one!

Mohs studied the appearance and properties of different minerals. He also published several works about minerals!

HALITE

MOHS SCALE OF HARDNESS

Some minerals are soft. Others are hard. Hard minerals scratch softer ones. Mohs created a scale. He chose ten minerals. He organized them by hardness, from one to ten.

Scientists still use Mohs's scale. They scratch unknown minerals with those Mohs organized. This tells the hardness of the unknown mineral. The hardness helps scientists identify the mineral.

FRIEDRICH MOHS

BORN: January 29, 1773, Gernrode, Germany

MARRIED: Josephine Fiala, 1828

CHILDREN: None

DIED: September 29, 1839, Agordo, Italy

MANY MINERALS

Earth has thousands of minerals. But most minerals are rare. Only about 100 minerals are commonly found. And fewer than 20 are common in rocks.

Still, new minerals are discovered every year. Minerals teach scientists about Earth's history. Scientists learn more about Earth all the time!

Gold

Some minerals can be harmful. Other minerals are found in dangerous places, such as caves. Mineralogists have to be careful!

IN THE FIELD

Mineralogists travel the world. They work in the field. They collect rock and mineral samples.

Some minerals are valuable, such as gold and diamond. These minerals are mined. Scientists help find them. Then, they help miners remove the minerals.

Some mineralogists help miners turn minerals into usable materials. Then, the materials can be used in industries such as construction.

IN THE LAB

Scientists also study the samples they collect. The minerals are **classified**. Scientists use many methods to do this.

Scientists look at a mineral's color and appearance. They measure its **density**. They find out if it is magnetic. They test it for **radioactivity**. They see how the mineral **reacts** to heat and chemicals. These tests help scientists learn about the mineral's properties.

A MINERALOGIST'S TOOL KIT

MAGNET
This tests how magnetic minerals are.

MAGNIFYING GLASS
This tool gives an up-close look at minerals. It shows tiny details.

Mineralogists use many tools to **classify** and study minerals.

PETROGRAPHIC MICROSCOPE
A special light is shined on minerals. The light affects minerals in different ways.

STREAK PLATE
Minerals are scratched on this plate. The color of the **streak** left behind identifies a mineral.

MINING AND BEYOND

Studying minerals is exciting! Many mineralogists get to travel around the world. They can also teach students about minerals.

Computers and other **technology** help scientists study minerals in new ways. Technology allows the study of minerals on other planets. Scientists use a device called the CheMin. It identifies minerals found on Mars!

Scientists have created machines similar to CheMin for use on Earth. Scientist David Blake uses one of these devices to study minerals on a Hawaiian volcano in 2008.

BECOME A MINERALOGIST!

Do you dream of becoming a mineralogist? Here are some things you can do now!

TAKE SCIENCE AND MATH CLASSES. Studying minerals involves math and science. Getting good grades in those classes now will help you in the future.

START A MINERAL COLLECTION. Pick up rocks when you're outside. Try to figure out what minerals might be in them. This is good practice!

ASK QUESTIONS! Scientists ask a lot of questions. They look for new ways to find answers. You can get started now!

TEST YOUR KNOWLEDGE

1. What do mineralogists study?

2. In what year was Friedrich Mohs born?

3. The CheMin studies minerals on Earth. TRUE OR FALSE?

THINK ABOUT IT!

Minerals are all around you! What are some minerals that you use every day?

ANSWERS: 1. Minerals 2. 1773 3. False

GLOSSARY

classify – to put things in groups according to their characteristics. Something sorted this way is classified.

density – the quantity of something per unit of area.

radioactivity – the giving off of rays of energy by the breaking apart of atoms of certain elements.

react – to change when mixed with another chemical or substance.

streak – a long, thin mark or stripe.

substance – anything that takes up space, such as a solid object or a liquid.

technology – a capability given by the practical application of knowledge.

unique (yoo-NEEK) – being the only one of its kind.